EMMANUEL JOSEPH

From Ballots to Boardrooms, The Role of Politics, Psychology, and Health in Business Strategy

Copyright © 2025 by Emmanuel Joseph

All rights reserved. No part of this publication may be reproduced, stored or transmitted in any form or by any means, electronic, mechanical, photocopying, recording, scanning, or otherwise without written permission from the publisher. It is illegal to copy this book, post it to a website, or distribute it by any other means without permission.

First edition

This book was professionally typeset on Reedsy. Find out more at reedsy.com

Contents

1	Chapter 1: Introduction	1
2	Chapter 2: Politics and Business: An Inextricable Link	3
3	Chapter 3: Political Systems and Their Impact on Business	5
4	Chapter 4: The Influence of Political Decisions on Market...	7
5	Chapter 5: Psychological Foundations in Business Strategy	9
6	Chapter 6: The Role of Cognitive Bias in Decision Making	11
7	Chapter 7: Organizational Behavior and Psychology	13
8	Chapter 8: Health and Productivity: An Underrated Duo	15
9	Chapter 9: Workplace Health Policies	17
10	Chapter 10: The Economics of Health in Business	19
11	Chapter 11: Integrating Politics, Psychology, and Health in...	21
12	Chapter 12: Case Studies of Political Influence in Business...	23
13	Chapter 13: Psychological Strategies for Effective...	25
14	Chapter 14: Health as a Business Strategy	27
15	Chapter 15: Challenges and Ethical Considerations	29
16	Chapter 16: Future Trends and Innovations	31
17	Chapter 17: Conclusion	33

1

Chapter 1: Introduction

In today's rapidly evolving business landscape, the intersection of politics, psychology, and health has become increasingly significant in shaping effective business strategies. While the influence of politics on business is well-documented, understanding the psychological underpinnings and health considerations can provide a comprehensive approach to navigating the complexities of the corporate world. This book aims to explore these critical dimensions and their interplay, offering insights and strategies for business leaders and professionals.

The journey from ballots to boardrooms is marked by the continuous interplay of political decisions and business strategies. Governments enact policies that shape market conditions, regulate industries, and influence consumer behavior. Business leaders must stay attuned to these political dynamics to make informed decisions and capitalize on opportunities. However, politics alone cannot account for the intricacies of effective business strategy.

Psychology, with its focus on human behavior and cognitive processes, plays a crucial role in decision-making, leadership, and organizational culture. Understanding psychological principles allows business leaders to harness the power of human capital, foster innovation, and create a positive work environment. By leveraging psychological insights, businesses can enhance employee engagement, improve productivity, and drive sustainable growth.

Health, often overlooked in the realm of business strategy, is an essential component of long-term success. A healthy workforce is more productive, innovative, and resilient. Integrating health considerations into business strategies can lead to improved employee well-being, reduced absenteeism, and enhanced organizational performance. Moreover, businesses that prioritize health can gain a competitive edge by attracting and retaining top talent.

As we embark on this exploration of the role of politics, psychology, and health in business strategy, it is essential to recognize the interconnectedness of these dimensions. By understanding their interplay, business leaders can develop holistic strategies that address the multifaceted challenges of the modern business environment. This book will provide a comprehensive framework for integrating political awareness, psychological insights, and health considerations into effective business strategies, ultimately driving sustainable success.

2

Chapter 2: Politics and Business: An Inextricable Link

Politics and business are two realms that have always been closely intertwined. The relationship between the two can be seen in how government policies shape business environments and how businesses, in turn, influence political processes. Understanding this intricate relationship is crucial for business leaders who aim to navigate the complexities of the modern economy successfully.

Political decisions can have far-reaching consequences on the business landscape. For example, changes in tax policies can affect corporate profitability and investment decisions. Regulatory frameworks can either facilitate or hinder business operations. Trade agreements and tariffs can impact supply chains and market access. In this chapter, we will explore how political systems and decisions influence business strategies and outcomes.

One significant aspect of this relationship is the role of government in creating a stable and predictable business environment. Political stability and the rule of law are essential for businesses to operate efficiently and make long-term investments. Political instability, on the other hand, can create uncertainty and risks that deter investment and economic growth. Business leaders must stay informed about political developments and assess their potential impact on their operations and strategies.

Moreover, businesses are not passive actors in the political arena. They actively engage in lobbying, advocacy, and political contributions to influence policy decisions. By doing so, they seek to shape regulations and policies in ways that favor their interests. This dynamic interaction between business and politics underscores the importance of understanding the political landscape and developing strategies to navigate it effectively.

3

Chapter 3: Political Systems and Their Impact on Business

Different political systems around the world create varying business environments. Democratic systems, authoritarian regimes, and hybrid political structures each have distinct characteristics that influence how businesses operate. In this chapter, we will examine the impact of different political systems on business strategy and performance.

In democratic systems, businesses operate in an environment characterized by transparency, accountability, and the rule of law. These systems typically provide a level playing field for businesses, with clear regulations and legal protections. However, the competitive nature of democratic politics can lead to frequent changes in policies, creating a dynamic environment that requires businesses to be agile and adaptable.

Authoritarian regimes, on the other hand, often provide a more stable but less transparent business environment. Decision-making processes are centralized, and businesses may benefit from close relationships with political leaders. However, the lack of transparency and accountability can create risks and uncertainties. Businesses operating in such environments must navigate complex power dynamics and be prepared for sudden changes in policies.

Hybrid political systems combine elements of democracy and authoritarianism. These systems can create unique challenges and opportunities for businesses. For example, some countries may have democratic institutions but authoritarian practices, leading to an unpredictable business environment. Understanding the nuances of hybrid systems is crucial for developing effective business strategies.

4

Chapter 4: The Influence of Political Decisions on Market Trends

Political decisions have a profound impact on market trends and business dynamics. Government policies, international relations, and geopolitical events can all shape market conditions and influence business strategies. In this chapter, we will explore how political decisions affect market trends and how businesses can respond to these changes.

One of the most significant ways political decisions influence market trends is through fiscal and monetary policies. Government spending, taxation, and central bank decisions can affect economic growth, inflation, and interest rates. Businesses must closely monitor these policies and adjust their strategies accordingly. For example, expansionary fiscal policies may create opportunities for growth, while contractionary policies may require cost-cutting measures.

International relations and trade policies also play a crucial role in shaping market trends. Trade agreements, tariffs, and sanctions can impact supply chains, market access, and competitive dynamics. Businesses must stay informed about geopolitical developments and assess their potential impact on their operations. Developing strategies to mitigate risks and capitalize on opportunities in the global market is essential for long-term success.

Geopolitical events, such as conflicts, elections, and diplomatic negotiations, can create significant volatility in markets. Businesses must be prepared to respond to sudden changes in market conditions and develop contingency plans to manage risks. Understanding the political landscape and its potential impact on market trends is crucial for making informed business decisions.

5

Chapter 5: Psychological Foundations in Business Strategy

Psychology is a vital component of effective business strategy. Understanding human behavior, decision-making processes, and cognitive biases can provide valuable insights for developing successful strategies. In this chapter, we will explore the psychological foundations that underpin business strategy and their implications for organizational success.

One key aspect of psychology in business strategy is the study of cognitive biases. Cognitive biases are systematic patterns of deviation from rationality in judgment and decision-making. These biases can significantly impact business decisions, leading to suboptimal outcomes. For example, confirmation bias can cause individuals to seek out information that supports their existing beliefs, while ignoring contradictory evidence. By recognizing and mitigating cognitive biases, business leaders can make more informed and rational decisions.

Another important area of psychology in business strategy is organizational behavior. Organizational behavior examines how individuals and groups interact within an organization. It encompasses topics such as motivation, leadership, communication, and team dynamics. Understanding organizational behavior allows business leaders to create a positive work environment, foster collaboration, and drive employee engagement. Effective leadership, clear communication, and a supportive organizational culture are essential for achieving business goals and sustaining long-term success.

6

Chapter 6: The Role of Cognitive Bias in Decision Making

Cognitive biases are inherent in human decision-making processes and can have a profound impact on business strategy. In this chapter, we will delve into the various cognitive biases that influence decision-making and explore strategies for mitigating their effects.

One common cognitive bias is the anchoring effect, where individuals rely heavily on the first piece of information they encounter when making decisions. This can lead to biased judgments and suboptimal outcomes. For example, an initial price estimate can anchor subsequent negotiations, even if the estimate is inaccurate. To mitigate the anchoring effect, business leaders should seek multiple perspectives, challenge initial assumptions, and consider a range of possibilities.

Another cognitive bias is the availability heuristic, where individuals assess the likelihood of events based on how easily examples come to mind. This can lead to overestimating the probability of rare but memorable events and underestimating the likelihood of common but less salient events. To counter the availability heuristic, business leaders should rely on data and evidence rather than anecdotal information. Analyzing historical trends and seeking diverse viewpoints can provide a more accurate assessment of risks and opportunities.

The overconfidence bias is another common cognitive bias that can impact business decision-making. Overconfidence can lead individuals to overestimate their abilities and underestimate risks, resulting in poor decisions. To address overconfidence, business leaders should encourage a culture of humility and openness to feedback. Seeking input from diverse perspectives and conducting rigorous risk assessments can help mitigate the effects of overconfidence.

7

Chapter 7: Organizational Behavior and Psychology

Organizational behavior is the study of how individuals and groups interact within an organization. Understanding organizational behavior is essential for developing effective business strategies and fostering a positive work environment. In this chapter, we will explore the key concepts of organizational behavior and their implications for business success.

Motivation is a central concept in organizational behavior. Motivated employees are more engaged, productive, and committed to achieving organizational goals. Various theories of motivation, such as Maslow's hierarchy of needs, Herzberg's two-factor theory, and self-determination theory, provide insights into what drives employee motivation. By understanding these theories, business leaders can design strategies to enhance employee motivation, such as providing meaningful work, recognizing achievements, and offering opportunities for growth and development.

Leadership is another critical aspect of organizational behavior. Effective leadership is essential for guiding and inspiring employees, fostering collaboration, and driving organizational success. Various leadership styles, such as transformational, transactional, and servant leadership, have different impacts on organizational behavior and outcomes. Business leaders should understand their leadership style, adapt it to different situations, and develop the skills needed to lead effectively.

Communication is a fundamental aspect of organizational behavior that influences how information is shared, understood, and acted upon within an organization. Effective communication fosters collaboration, reduces misunderstandings, and enhances decision-making. Business leaders should prioritize clear and open communication, create channels for feedback, and ensure that information flows smoothly across the organization.

Team dynamics are also crucial in organizational behavior. High-performing teams exhibit characteristics such as trust, collaboration, and a shared sense of purpose. Understanding the factors that influence team dynamics, such as group cohesion, role clarity, and conflict resolution, can help business leaders build and maintain effective teams. By fostering a positive team environment, business leaders can enhance productivity, creativity, and overall organizational performance.

8

Chapter 8: Health and Productivity: An Underrated Duo

Health and productivity are closely linked, yet the importance of health in business strategy is often overlooked. A healthy workforce is more productive, engaged, and resilient, leading to improved organizational performance. In this chapter, we will explore the relationship between health and productivity and discuss strategies for integrating health considerations into business strategy.

Employee health has a direct impact on productivity. Healthy employees are less likely to take sick leave, experience burnout, or suffer from chronic illnesses. This translates to fewer absences, higher energy levels, and greater focus on work tasks. Investing in employee health through wellness programs, preventive care, and a supportive work environment can lead to significant gains in productivity and overall organizational success.

Mental health is a critical component of employee well-being and productivity. Stress, anxiety, and depression can negatively affect employee performance, job satisfaction, and retention. Business leaders should prioritize mental health by promoting a culture of openness, providing access to mental health resources, and offering support through employee assistance programs. Creating a psychologically safe workplace where employees feel valued and supported can enhance mental well-being and productivity.

Workplace health policies play a crucial role in promoting employee health and productivity. Implementing policies that address physical health, such as ergonomic workstations, regular breaks, and access to healthy food options, can reduce the risk of workplace injuries and illnesses. Additionally, policies that support work-life balance, such as flexible work arrangements and paid time off, can help employees manage stress and maintain overall well-being. By prioritizing health in business strategy, organizations can create a healthier and more productive workforce.

9

Chapter 9: Workplace Health Policies

Workplace health policies are essential for promoting employee well-being and enhancing organizational performance. By implementing effective health policies, businesses can create a supportive work environment that fosters physical and mental health. In this chapter, we will explore various workplace health policies and their impact on business strategy.

One key aspect of workplace health policies is the promotion of physical health. Businesses can implement policies that encourage regular physical activity, provide access to healthy food options, and create ergonomic workstations. For example, offering gym memberships, organizing fitness challenges, and providing nutritious snacks can contribute to employee well-being. Additionally, ergonomic workstations can reduce the risk of musculoskeletal disorders and enhance comfort and productivity.

Mental health policies are equally important for creating a supportive work environment. Businesses can promote mental health by offering employee assistance programs, providing access to counseling services, and fostering a culture of openness and support. Encouraging employees to take regular breaks, manage stress, and seek help when needed can contribute to a healthier and more productive workforce. By prioritizing mental health, businesses can reduce absenteeism, improve job satisfaction, and enhance overall performance.

Work-life balance is another critical aspect of workplace health policies. Flexible work arrangements, such as remote work, flexible hours, and job-sharing, can help employees manage their personal and professional responsibilities. Providing paid time off, encouraging vacations, and respecting employees' boundaries outside of work hours are also essential for promoting work-life balance. By supporting work-life balance, businesses can enhance employee well-being, reduce burnout, and improve retention.

10

Chapter 10: The Economics of Health in Business

The economics of health in business is a critical consideration for developing effective strategies. Investing in employee health can yield significant returns in terms of productivity, performance, and cost savings. In this chapter, we will explore the economic implications of health in business and discuss strategies for maximizing the benefits of health investments.

One of the most significant economic benefits of investing in employee health is the reduction in healthcare costs. By promoting preventive care, wellness programs, and healthy lifestyle choices, businesses can reduce the incidence of chronic illnesses and associated healthcare expenses. For example, providing access to regular health screenings, vaccinations, and wellness coaching can help identify and address health issues early, preventing costly medical interventions down the line.

Productivity gains are another key economic benefit of investing in employee health. Healthy employees are more engaged, focused, and motivated, leading to higher levels of productivity. By reducing absenteeism and presenteeism (when employees are present but not fully productive due to health issues), businesses can enhance overall performance and achieve their goals more efficiently. Investing in health can also lead to improved job satisfaction and employee morale, further contributing to productivity gains.

Attracting and retaining top talent is another economic advantage of prioritizing health in business strategy. In today's competitive job market, employees seek employers who prioritize their well-being and offer comprehensive health benefits. By providing robust health programs, businesses can attract high-quality candidates and reduce turnover. Investing in employee health can also enhance the employer brand and reputation, making the organization more attractive to potential employees and customers.

11

Chapter 11: Integrating Politics, Psychology, and Health in Business Strategy

Integrating politics, psychology, and health into business strategy can provide a comprehensive and holistic approach to achieving organizational success. By understanding and leveraging the interconnectedness of these dimensions, business leaders can develop strategies that address the multifaceted challenges of the modern business environment. In this chapter, we will explore how to integrate politics, psychology, and health into business strategy effectively.

One key aspect of integrating politics into business strategy is staying informed about political developments and assessing their potential impact on the organization. Business leaders should monitor government policies, regulatory changes, and geopolitical events to make informed decisions. Developing relationships with policymakers, engaging in advocacy, and participating in industry associations can also help businesses influence policy decisions and create a favorable business environment.

Psychology plays a crucial role in shaping organizational behavior, leadership, and decision-making. By understanding psychological principles, business leaders can enhance employee motivation, improve communication, and foster a positive organizational culture. Integrating psychological insights into business strategy involves promoting a culture of openness, providing opportunities for growth and development, and recognizing and addressing cognitive biases in decision-making processes.

Health considerations should be a central component of business strategy. By prioritizing employee health, businesses can enhance productivity, reduce healthcare costs, and improve overall performance. Integrating health into business strategy involves implementing comprehensive health programs, promoting work-life balance, and fostering a supportive work environment. Business leaders should also regularly assess the effectiveness of health initiatives and make adjustments as needed to ensure continuous improvement.

12

Chapter 12: Case Studies of Political Influence in Business Success

C ase studies provide valuable insights into the impact of political influence on business success. By examining real-world examples, business leaders can learn from the experiences of others and develop strategies to navigate political dynamics effectively. In this chapter, we will explore several case studies that highlight the role of politics in shaping business outcomes.

One notable case study is the influence of government policies on the renewable energy industry. In many countries, government incentives, subsidies, and regulations have played a critical role in promoting the growth of renewable energy businesses. For example, the introduction of feed-in tariffs, tax credits, and renewable energy mandates has created favorable market conditions for solar, wind, and other renewable energy companies. These political decisions have enabled businesses to invest in renewable energy projects, innovate, and achieve significant growth.

Another case study examines the impact of trade policies on the automotive industry. Trade agreements, tariffs, and import/export regulations have a profound influence on the global automotive market. For instance, the implementation of tariffs on imported steel and aluminum can increase production costs for automakers, affecting their profitability and pricing strategies. Conversely, trade agreements that reduce tariffs and promote free trade can create opportunities for automakers to expand their markets and increase competitiveness.

A third case study explores the role of lobbying and advocacy in shaping business success. Businesses often engage in lobbying to influence policy decisions and create a favorable regulatory environment. For example, the pharmaceutical industry has historically invested significant resources in lobbying efforts to shape healthcare policies, drug pricing regulations, and patent protections. These lobbying efforts have had a substantial impact on the industry's profitability and market dynamics.

13

Chapter 13: Psychological Strategies for Effective Leadership

Effective leadership is essential for guiding organizations to success. Psychological strategies can enhance leadership effectiveness by leveraging insights into human behavior, motivation, and communication. In this chapter, we will explore various psychological strategies that business leaders can use to inspire and lead their teams effectively.

One key psychological strategy for effective leadership is the use of transformational leadership. Transformational leaders inspire and motivate their followers by creating a compelling vision, fostering a sense of purpose, and encouraging innovation. They build strong relationships with their team members, provide support and recognition, and empower individuals to achieve their full potential. By adopting a transformational leadership style, business leaders can enhance employee engagement, creativity, and performance.

Another important strategy is the practice of emotional intelligence. Emotional intelligence involves the ability to recognize, understand, and manage one's own emotions and the emotions of others. Leaders with high emotional intelligence are better equipped to navigate interpersonal relationships, resolve conflicts, and build trust with their team members.

Developing emotional intelligence requires self-awareness, empathy, and effective communication skills. By cultivating emotional intelligence, business leaders can create a positive and supportive work environment.

Effective communication is a critical psychological strategy for leadership. Clear, transparent, and open communication fosters trust, reduces misunderstandings, and enhances collaboration. Leaders should prioritize active listening, provide constructive feedback, and ensure that information flows smoothly within the organization. By promoting a culture of open communication, leaders can create an environment where employees feel valued, heard, and motivated.

14

Chapter 14: Health as a Business Strategy

Health is a vital component of business strategy that can drive organizational success. By prioritizing employee health and well-being, businesses can enhance productivity, reduce costs, and improve overall performance. In this chapter, we will explore how health can be integrated into business strategy and the benefits it can bring.

One key aspect of integrating health into business strategy is the implementation of comprehensive wellness programs. Wellness programs can include a range of initiatives such as fitness challenges, health screenings, mental health support, and nutrition education. These programs promote healthy behaviors, prevent chronic illnesses, and enhance overall well-being. By investing in wellness programs, businesses can create a healthier and more productive workforce.

Another important consideration is the promotion of mental health in the workplace. Mental health is a critical component of overall well-being and productivity. Businesses should provide access to mental health resources, promote a culture of openness, and offer support through employee assistance programs. Encouraging employees to take regular breaks, manage stress, and seek help when needed can contribute to a healthier and more resilient workforce.

Work-life balance is also essential for promoting employee health and well-being. Flexible work arrangements, such as remote work and flexible hours, can help employees manage their personal and professional responsibilities. Providing paid time off, encouraging vacations, and respecting employees' boundaries outside of work hours are also important for promoting work-life balance. By supporting work-life balance, businesses can reduce burnout, enhance job satisfaction, and improve retention.

15

Chapter 15: Challenges and Ethical Considerations

Integrating politics, psychology, and health into business strategy presents several challenges and ethical considerations. Business leaders must navigate these complexities to develop effective and responsible strategies. In this chapter, we will explore some of the key challenges and ethical considerations associated with integrating these dimensions into business strategy.

One significant challenge is balancing short-term and long-term goals. Business leaders may face pressure to achieve immediate results, but integrating politics, psychology, and health into strategy often requires long-term investments and planning. Balancing short-term and long-term goals requires careful prioritization, effective communication, and a commitment to sustainable practices.

Ethical considerations are also paramount when integrating politics into business strategy. Businesses must navigate the complexities of lobbying, advocacy, and political contributions while maintaining transparency and accountability. Ensuring that business practices align with ethical standards and avoiding conflicts of interest are essential for maintaining public trust and credibility.

Another challenge is addressing the complexities of integrating psychological insights into business strategy. While understanding human behavior can provide valuable insights, it also raises ethical questions about manipulation and influence. Business leaders must navigate these ethical considerations by promoting transparency, fairness, and respect for individuals' autonomy. Ensuring that psychological strategies are used ethically and responsibly is crucial for maintaining a positive organizational culture and reputation.

Health-related challenges and ethical considerations also arise when integrating health into business strategy. Businesses must balance the need for employee health and well-being with the financial constraints and operational demands of the organization. Ethical considerations include ensuring that health programs are inclusive, accessible, and respectful of employees' privacy and autonomy. Business leaders should prioritize transparency, fairness, and employee engagement in the development and implementation of health initiatives.

16

Chapter 16: Future Trends and Innovations

The business landscape is continuously evolving, and staying ahead of future trends and innovations is crucial for long-term success. In this chapter, we will explore emerging trends and innovations in the realms of politics, psychology, and health that are likely to shape business strategy in the coming years.

In the political sphere, businesses will need to navigate the increasing complexity of global geopolitics. Trade tensions, geopolitical conflicts, and shifting alliances will continue to impact market conditions and supply chains. Businesses must stay informed about geopolitical developments and develop strategies to mitigate risks and capitalize on opportunities. Additionally, the rise of digital technologies and social media will influence political processes and public opinion, creating new challenges and opportunities for businesses.

Psychological trends and innovations will also play a significant role in shaping business strategy. Advances in artificial intelligence, machine learning, and behavioral economics will provide new tools for understanding and influencing human behavior. Businesses can leverage these technologies to enhance decision-making, personalize customer experiences, and optimize organizational performance. However, ethical considerations related to data privacy, transparency, and bias must be carefully addressed.

Health-related trends and innovations will continue to transform the business landscape. The growing focus on mental health, wellness, and preventive care will drive the development of new health programs and initiatives. Businesses can leverage technology, such as wearable devices and telehealth, to promote employee health and well-being. Additionally, the integration of health considerations into corporate social responsibility (CSR) initiatives will become increasingly important, as businesses seek to create positive social and environmental impacts.

17

Chapter 17: Conclusion

As we conclude our exploration of the role of politics, psychology, and health in business strategy, it is essential to recognize the interconnectedness of these dimensions and their impact on organizational success. By understanding and leveraging the interplay between politics, psychology, and health, business leaders can develop comprehensive and holistic strategies that address the multifaceted challenges of the modern business environment.

The journey from ballots to boardrooms is marked by the continuous interaction between political decisions, psychological insights, and health considerations. By staying informed about political developments, recognizing cognitive biases, and prioritizing employee health, businesses can navigate the complexities of the corporate world effectively. Integrating these dimensions into business strategy provides a framework for achieving sustainable growth, enhancing productivity, and fostering a positive organizational culture.

As we look to the future, the evolving business landscape will present new challenges and opportunities. Staying ahead of emerging trends and innovations in politics, psychology, and health will be crucial for long-term success. By embracing a holistic approach to business strategy, business leaders can create resilient, adaptable, and thriving organizations that drive positive impacts for employees, customers, and society.

From Ballots to Boardrooms: The Role of Politics, Psychology, and

Health in Business Strategy

Description:

In the ever-evolving landscape of modern business, understanding the intricate interplay between politics, psychology, and health is essential for developing effective strategies. "From Ballots to Boardrooms: The Role of Politics, Psychology, and Health in Business Strategy" explores these critical dimensions and their impact on organizational success.

This comprehensive book delves into the dynamic relationship between politics and business, examining how government policies, regulatory frameworks, and geopolitical events shape market trends and business environments. It highlights the importance of staying informed about political developments and engaging in advocacy to navigate the complexities of the corporate world.

The psychological foundations of business strategy are explored in depth, with a focus on cognitive biases, organizational behavior, and effective leadership. By leveraging psychological insights, business leaders can enhance decision-making, foster innovation, and create a positive work environment. The book provides valuable strategies for recognizing and mitigating cognitive biases, understanding organizational dynamics, and cultivating emotional intelligence.

Health is often an overlooked aspect of business strategy, yet it plays a crucial role in productivity and long-term success. The book underscores the importance of employee health and well-being, discussing workplace health policies, wellness programs, and the economics of health in business. By prioritizing health, businesses can reduce healthcare costs, enhance employee engagement, and improve overall performance.

"From Ballots to Boardrooms" integrates these dimensions into a holistic framework for business strategy. Through case studies, real-world examples, and practical insights, the book offers a comprehensive guide for business leaders to develop strategies that address the multifaceted challenges of the modern business environment. It emphasizes the interconnectedness of politics, psychology, and health, providing a roadmap for achieving sustainable growth, enhancing productivity, and fostering a positive organizational culture.

Ideal for business leaders, professionals, and anyone interested in the intersection of politics, psychology, and health, this book offers a wealth of knowledge and actionable strategies to navigate the complexities of the corporate world and drive organizational success.